Giraffes

by Barbara Keevil Parker

Lerner Publications Company • Minneapolis

To Samantha and Bridget

I want to express my appreciation to Carol Hinz for her editorial expertise. Thanks to my husband, Duane, for his constant encouragement.

The photographs in this book are used with the permission of: © John Kreul, p. 4; © Kari Weiss/Photo Network, p. 6; © W. Anderson/Root Resources, pp. 7, 8, 27, 32, 37; © Richard G. Fisher/Root Resources, pp. 9, 17, 25, 30; © Michele Burgess, pp. 10, 11, 12, 13, 14, 15, 16, 18, 19, 20, 22, 23, 26, 28, 31, 34, 39, 40, 42, 46–47; © Ted Farrington/Root Resources, p. 21; © Robert Grubbs/Photo Network, p. 24; © Connie Bransilver/Photo Researchers, Inc., p. 29; © Mary and Lloyd McCarthy/Root Resources, p. 33; PhotoDisc Royalty Free by Getty Images, p. 35; © Gary Kramer, p. 36; © Jonathan Blair/CORBIS, p. 38; © Wolfgang Kaehler/CORBIS, p. 41; © Earl L. Kubis/Root Resources, p. 43.

Front Cover: © W. Anderson/Root Resources

Lerner Publications Company
A division of Lerner Publishing Group
241 First Avenue North
Minneapolis, Minnesota 55401 U.S.A.

Website address: www.lernerbooks.com

Library of Congress Cataloging-in-Publication Data

Parker, Barbara Keevil.
    Giraffes / written by Barbara Keevil Parker.
       p.   cm. — (Early bird nature books)
    Includes index.
    ISBN: 0–8225–2419–8 (lib. bdg. : alk. paper)
    1. Giraffe—Juvenile literature. I. Title. II. Series.
QL737.U56P37 2005
599.638—dc22   2004006598

Manufactured in the United States of America
1 2 3 4 5 6 – JR – 10 09 08 07 06 05

Contents

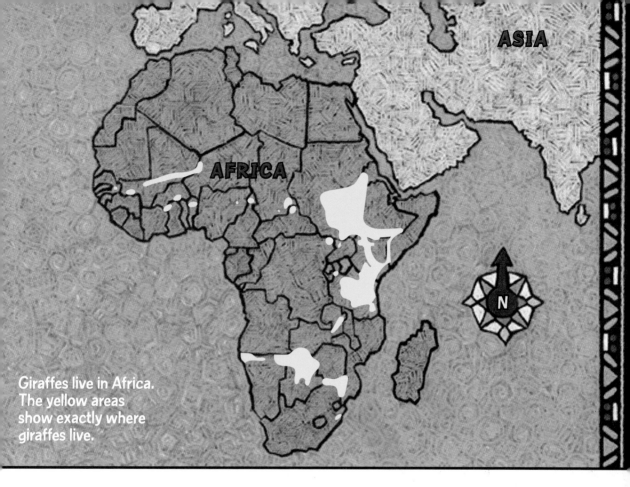

ASIA

AFRICA

N

Giraffes live in Africa.
The yellow areas
show exactly where
giraffes live.

Be a Word Detective

Can you find these words as you read about the giraffe's life? Be a detective and try to figure out what they mean. You can turn to the glossary on page 46 for help.

acacia	habitat	parks
browsing	herds	predators
calf	hoof	ruminants
cud	necking	vertebrae
extinct	nursing	

Chapter 1

This giraffe's tongue is 18 inches long. How tall are giraffes?

The Tallest Animal

Giraffes are the world's tallest animals. They have long legs and long necks. They even have long tongues. Everything about them is big.

Giraffes are 14 to 18 feet tall. A male may weigh 3,000 pounds or more. That's as much as a pickup truck! Female giraffes are a little smaller than males.

A giraffe's legs are 5 or 6 feet tall. That's as tall as your mom or dad. Long legs help giraffes run fast. Giraffes have a hoof at the end of each leg. A hoof is like a big, thick toenail that protects a giraffe's foot.

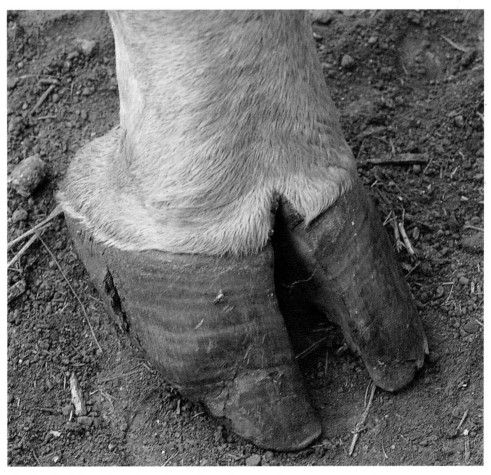

A giraffe's hoof is the size of a dinner plate.

Giraffes are tall enough to look through a building's second-floor windows.

A giraffe's neck is 5 or 6 feet long. Its neck has the same number of bones as your neck. Neck bones are called vertebrae (VUHR-tuh-bray). Your neck has seven vertebrae that are each 2 inches long. A giraffe has seven vertebrae that are each about 10 inches long.

A giraffe has bumps on its forehead. A female giraffe has two bumps. A male may have as many as five. These bumps look a little like horns. They are covered with skin and hair.

This giraffe's head has three bumps. Three bumps mean the giraffe is a male.

A giraffe's tail is about 6 feet long. Its tail has thick hair at the end. Each tail hair is thicker than 10 strands of your hair.

Giraffes swish their tails to keep away flies and other bugs.

The scientific name for the giraffe is Giraffa camelopardalis.

A giraffe has short fur all over its body. The fur is light-colored with darker spots. All giraffes have spots. But each giraffe's spots are different. Some spots are big, and some are small. Some are dark brown, and some are light brown. People who work with giraffes can tell them apart by their spots.

This leopard is a giraffe enemy.

Giraffes' spots have a job to do. Spots make giraffes hard to see. When a giraffe stands next to bushes or trees, its spots blend in with the shadows and sunlight. Spots help giraffes hide from predators (PREH-duh-turz). Predators hunt and eat other animals. Lions, leopards, and hyenas are predators that hunt giraffes.

Giraffes also have other ways to stay safe from predators. Their ears help them listen for danger. Their big eyes can see up to 1 mile away. When giraffes see a predator coming, they use their long legs to run!

A giraffe's top speed is almost 35 miles an hour.

Chapter 2

Giraffes and zebras live in the same part of the world. Where do giraffes live?

Eating and Drinking

 Giraffes live in eastern and southern Africa. Some giraffes also live in parts of central and western Africa.

A habitat is the place where an animal lives. The giraffe's habitat is the hot, dry African savanna. A savanna is a flat, grassy area with a few trees and shrubs. Acacia (uh-KAY-shuh) and combretum (kom-BREE-tum) trees are common. The savanna also has water holes where giraffes and other animals can drink.

The African savanna is filled with many kinds of tall grasses.

The savanna is filled with food for giraffes. The way giraffes eat is called browsing. They nibble at leaves, twigs, bark, and other plants.

Giraffes also eat seeds and fruits. A lot of their food comes from tall trees. Sometimes they eat leaves from bushes. Each day, a giraffe eats about 75 pounds of food.

A giraffe's long neck helps it to reach leaves high in the trees.

Thick skin on the giraffe's tongue protects it from thorns on the acacia tree.

Giraffes' favorite food is the leaves of the acacia tree. Acacias are tall trees with sharp thorns. A giraffe stretches its neck to reach the highest branches. It uses its long tongue to pull branches and leaves into its mouth.

Giraffes are ruminants (ROO-muh-nuhnts). Ruminants are animals that have more than one stomach. Giraffes and many other ruminants have four stomachs. Their extra stomachs help them to break down their food.

Sometimes a giraffe uses its neck to reach low bushes.

Giraffes spend many hours chewing cud.

A giraffe doesn't chew much before it swallows. Later, it brings food back up its throat and into its mouth to chew it some more. The food that comes back up is called a cud. The cud is about the size of a baseball. A giraffe chews the cud, then swallows it again.

Giraffes don't need to drink much water.
The leaves they eat have water in them.
A giraffe can go without drinking for more than
one week. But on a hot day, a giraffe may
drink as much as 10 gallons of water.

In one week, a giraffe may drink two gallons of water.
That's as much as two big jugs of milk.

Giraffes do not stand in the water. Their hooves might get stuck in the mud.

For giraffes, drinking water is tricky. Giraffes are so tall that they have a hard time reaching water on the ground. To drink, a giraffe must spread its front feet wide apart. Or it must bend its knees. That is the only way its mouth can reach the water.

Getting a drink can also be dangerous. A giraffe cannot watch out for predators when its head is down. Lions and other predators wait at water holes. When a giraffe is drinking, predators may attack. If a predator comes, a giraffe must stand up very fast. Then it can run away.

Lions come to a water hole to drink. They also come to hunt giraffes.

Chapter 3

These giraffes are in a group. What is a group of giraffes called?

Giraffe Talk

Giraffes live together in groups called herds. Herds have 12 to 16 giraffes. Giraffes do not stay with one herd. They come and go from one herd to another.

A giraffe may grunt if it is surprised.

Giraffes are quiet animals. Most of the time, they don't make any sounds. But sometimes they grunt, cough, growl, or snore. Other times, giraffes use movements to talk to each other.

A giraffe uses its big ears to listen for danger.

When a giraffe sees danger, it holds its neck straight up. It may stand still, turn its head, and stare. Or it may paw the ground with its front feet and switch its tail back and forth. It might also snort to warn other giraffes.

Young male giraffes use their necks to talk to each other. One giraffe rubs its head or neck against the head or neck of another. This is called necking. Necking helps young male giraffes test which one has a stronger neck.

A young male giraffe rubs its neck against another male giraffe that is the same age.

These adult males use their heads and necks to fight.

Sometimes adult male giraffes fight with their necks. They fight to see who is boss. Two males stand side by side. One giraffe swings his head and neck. He hits his head against the other giraffe. Then the other giraffe takes a turn. After 10 or 20 minutes of fighting, one giraffe walks away. He has lost the fight.

Chapter 4

This baby giraffe is only 3 days old. How much does a baby giraffe weigh?

Baby Giraffes

A baby giraffe is called a calf. A baby giraffe is 6 feet tall when it is born. That's the size of a grown man.

You weighed about 6 to 10 pounds at birth. Baby giraffes weigh 120 to 150 pounds. That is as much as an adult human weighs!

Baby giraffes are born head first. A mother giraffe stands up while giving birth. When her calf is born, it falls 6 feet to the ground. But the fall doesn't hurt the calf.

This calf has just been born. It will stand up and walk in less than one hour.

The mother licks her new calf. Then she helps it to stand. The calf needs to start walking right away so that it will be safe from predators. Predators know the smell of a newborn calf. When a mother and her calf walk away, they leave the smell behind.

A mother giraffe licks her calf to keep it clean.

A calf grows quickly. After one year, it will be about 9 feet tall!

Newborn giraffes drink milk from their mother. This is called nursing. After six weeks, young giraffes begin nibbling on leaves. But they also keep nursing from their mother. Calves stop drinking milk by the time they are one year old.

Sometimes one mother watches many calves. The other mothers will come back later.

Calves and their mothers live in herds with other mothers and calves. Herds keep them safe. Each herd member watches for danger. If a giraffe sees a predator coming near, the giraffe warns the others.

A mother and her calf do not stay with just one herd. They may live with one herd of giraffes for a few days. Then they will move to be with a different herd.

This mother and calf can use their good eyesight to find a herd with other mothers and calves.

When a male giraffe is about three years old, he leaves his mother. He may live alone. Or he may join other young males. Males move from herd to herd either alone or together.

This calf's mother can call it by making a mooing noise.

The young giraffe on the right is almost full grown.

A female giraffe stays with her mother until she is four years old. At the age of four, females are old enough to start their own families. Most males wait until they are around seven years old.

Most wild giraffes live 15 or 20 years. A few live to be 25 years old.

Chapter 5

People travel to Africa to take pictures of giraffes. Where are giraffes safe from hunters?

Giraffes and People

Many years ago, hunters came to Africa and killed thousands of giraffes. After a while, people realized there weren't many giraffes left. People began to worry that giraffes might become extinct. When an animal is extinct, it is gone forever.

To help the giraffes, people set up special parks. Hunters cannot hunt in these parks. Giraffes and other animals are safe there. People also made new laws to protect giraffes. The laws make sure giraffes outside of parks are safe too.

This giraffe is in a park. A worker at the park feeds the giraffe.

Giraffes are too tall to walk under these telephone wires.

Humans still cause problems for giraffes. Telephone and electrical wires have been put up in giraffe habitat. The wires are not high enough for giraffes to walk under.

If a giraffe walks into a wire, it can get hurt. But people are learning to raise the wires. Giraffes can walk underneath higher wires.

These giraffes live in a park. They are safe from electrical wires and other dangers.

Farmers and giraffes don't always have an easy time sharing the same land.

Farmers also want to use the land where giraffes live. African farmers cut the trees and shrubs. They grow crops and raise cattle on giraffe habitat. Fewer trees and shrubs mean less food for giraffes. Without food, giraffes will starve and die.

Some cattle farmers let giraffes browse on their land. They do not mind because the giraffes only eat from trees and bushes. Giraffes don't eat the grass that the cattle eat.

These African cattle live in the same area as giraffes.

More and more people are taking over the land. They are building villages, cities, houses, and roads in places where giraffes used to live. That means there is less space for giraffes. Someday the parks might be the only place left for giraffes to live.

These giraffes are next to a road. Giraffes are sometimes killed by cars and trucks.

These giraffes are safe from danger. They live in a zoo.

People can visit giraffes in zoos across the globe. With protection from zoos and parks, giraffes will never be gone from this world.

On Sharing a Book

As you know, adults greatly influence a child's attitude toward reading. When a child sees you read, or when you share a book with a child, you're sending a message that reading is important. Show the child that reading a book together is important to you. Find a comfortable, quiet place. Turn off the television and limit other distractions, such as telephone calls.

Be prepared to start slowly. Take turns reading parts of this book. Stop and talk about what you're reading. Talk about the photographs. You may find that much of the shared time is spent discussing just a few pages. This discussion time is valuable for both of you, so don't move through the book too quickly. If the child begins to lose interest, stop reading. Continue sharing the book at another time. When you do pick up the book again, be sure to revisit the parts you have already read. Most importantly, enjoy the book!

Be a Vocabulary Detective

You will find a word list on page 5. Words selected for this list are important to the understanding of the topic of this book. Encourage the child to be a word detective and search for the words as you read the book together. Talk about what the words mean and how they are used in the sentence. Do any of these words have more than one meaning? You will find these words defined in a glossary on page 46.

What about Questions?

Use questions to make sure the child understands the information in this book. Here are some suggestions:

> What did this paragraph tell us? What does this picture show? What do you think we'll learn about next? Where do giraffes live? Could a giraffe live in your backyard? Why/Why not? What do giraffes eat? What are some dangers to giraffes? What do you think it's like being a giraffe? What is your favorite part of the book? Why?

If the child has questions, don't hesitate to respond with questions of your own, such as What do *you* think? Why? What is it that you don't know? If the child can't remember certain facts, turn to the index.

Introducing the Index

The index is an important learning tool. It helps readers get information quickly without searching throughout the whole book. Turn to the index on page 47. Choose an entry such as *tongues* and ask the child to use the index to find out how giraffes' tongues are special. Repeat this exercise with as many entries as you like. Ask the child to point out the differences between an index and a glossary. (The index helps readers find information quickly, while the glossary tells readers what words mean.)

Where in the World?

Many plants and animals found in the Early Bird Nature Books series live in parts of the world other than the United States. Encourage the child to find the places mentioned in this book on a world map or globe. Take time to talk about climate, terrain, and how you might live in such places.

All the World in Metric!

Although our monetary system is in metric units (based on multiples of 10), the United States is one of the few countries in the world that does not use the metric system of measurement. Here are some conversion activities you and the child can do using a calculator:

WHEN YOU KNOW:	MULTIPLY BY:	TO FIND:
miles	1.609	kilometers
feet	0.3048	meters
inches	2.54	centimeters
gallons	3.785	liters
tons	0.907	metric tons
pounds	0.454	kilograms

Activities

Write a story about a giraffe. Draw or paint pictures to go with your story. Design your own pattern for your giraffe's spots so you can identify it.

On a wall or door frame, mark your height. Cut a piece of string the same length as your height. Then cut a piece of string 15 feet long. That's the average size of a giraffe. Compare your height with the giraffe's height.

Glossary

acacia (uh-KAY-shuh): a thorny tree that grows in Africa

browsing: eating leaves, twigs, bark, and other plant parts

calf: a baby giraffe

cud: a lump of food a giraffe brings up from its stomach to chew again

extinct: no members of a kind of animal are still living

habitat: the place where an animal normally lives and grows

herds: groups of giraffes

hoof: the hard covering on a giraffe's foot

necking: when giraffes rub or bang their necks against each other

nursing: drinking mother's milk

parks: places where wild animals cannot be hunted

predators (PREH-duh-turz): animals that hunt and eat other animals

ruminants (ROO-muh-nuhnts): animals that chew cuds and have more than one stomach. Cows, deer, and giraffes are all ruminants.

vertebrae (VUHR-tuh-bray): bones that support and give shape to the neck and back

Index

Pages listed in **bold** type refer to photographs.

About the Author

Barbara Keevil Parker has shared her love and knowledge of wildlife through classroom visits and articles for children's magazines. She enjoys observing animals while hiking at Mount Ranier, visiting national parks, or when sitting on the porch in her backyard. A native of Washington State, she lives in Everett with her husband Duane. Barbara is an instructor at the Institute of Children's Literature and a member of the Society of Children's Book Writers and Illustrators. She is the author of several children's books.